Hologram Harry

Maverick
Early Readers

'Hologram Harry'
An original concept by Cath Jones
© Cath Jones 2022

Illustrated by Marina Pérez Luque

Published by MAVERICK ARTS PUBLISHING LTD
Studio 11, City Business Centre, 6 Brighton Road,
Horsham, West Sussex, RH13 5BB
© Maverick Arts Publishing Limited February 2022
+44 (0)1403 256941

A CIP catalogue record for this book is available at the British Library.

ISBN 978-1-84886-853-3

www.maverickbooks.co.uk

This book is rated as: Orange Band (Guided Reading)
It follows the requirements for Phase 5 phonics.
Most words are decodable, and any non-decodable words are familiar,
supported by the context and/or represented in the artwork.

Hologram Harry

illustrated by
Marina Pérez Luque

by **Cath Jones**

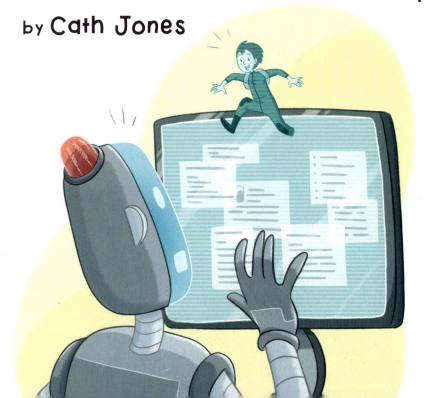

It was Friday afternoon. All week, Finn's class had been learning about holograms. "Here is your homework!" said his robot teacher. "I want you to make a hologram."

Finn grinned happily.

He couldn't wait to start!

Everyone grabbed their hologram homework kits. Then they got on the space shuttle to go home.

"This is the best homework
we've ever had!" said Finn.
Everyone agreed.

Soon, Finn got back home to his space pod.

His cat, Dodger, was waiting for him.

"I'm going to make the best hologram ever!"
Finn told Dodger. "Do you want to help?"

Together, they unpacked the hologram kit.

Finn worked for hours. Tap, tap, tap!

He typed away at the computer.

There was so much to think about.

Should it be a funny hologram?

What should it wear?

Finally, Finn was finished.

He pressed 'go' on the hologram kit.

POP! A tiny hologram person appeared.

"Hi! I'm Harry," it said.

"Meow!"

Dodger chased the mouse-sized hologram!

Harry ran away.

"Come back!" yelled Finn. "You're my homework!"

On Monday, Finn's classroom was full of exciting holograms. Finn was sad that he had no hologram to share.

But when the robot teacher switched on her computer...

...POP! Harry appeared! He jumped
onto the teacher's head, and then ran
out of the room.

Finn and his classmates chased after Harry. But the hologram vanished into the school computer network.

Whenever a computer was turned on,
Harry popped out!

"You need to catch your homework,"
said the robot teacher.

When the headteacher turned on her computer, Harry popped out dressed as a ballerina!

"Catch that hologram!" cried the

headteacher.

Harry popped out in the school kitchen. He hurled fish fingers and chips into the air.

Finn's homework was out of control!

"Catch that hologram!" cried the cook. But Harry was too fast for Finn and his friends.

Suddenly, Finn had an idea. Maybe a hologram cat like Dodger would help! Tap, tap, tap! Finn made a new hologram on his tablet.

The next time Harry popped out, so did

Computer Cat!

Harry looked worried. Would

Computer Cat chase him?

But instead, Computer Cat purred!

Harry stroked Computer Cat's fur
and smiled.

Now that Harry was standing still,

Finn could catch him in his tablet.

From now on, they could all

play happily together.

The robot teacher gave Finn top marks for his hologram homework.

"We're learning about robots next," said the teacher.

Finn couldn't wait to start his

robot homework!

Quiz

1. What was the name of Finn's cat?
a) Runner
b) Dodger
c) Chaser

2. What button did Finn press on the hologram kit?
a) Stop
b) Start
c) Go

3. What did Harry dress up as?
a) An astronaut
b) A ballerina
c) A policeman

4. What hologram did Finn make to catch Harry?
a) Computer Mouse
b) Digital Dog
c) Computer Cat

5. What will Finn be learning about next?
a) Robots
b) Tablets
c) Hologram kits

Turn over for answers

Book Bands for Guided Reading

The Institute of Education book banding system is a scale of colours that reflects the various levels of reading difficulty. The bands are assigned by taking into account the content, the language style, the layout and phonics. Word, phrase and sentence level work is also taken into consideration.

Maverick Early Readers are a bright, attractive range of books covering the pink to white bands. All of these books have been book banded for guided reading to the industry standard and edited by a leading educational consultant.

Pink
Red
Yellow
Blue
Green
Orange
Turquoise
Purple
Gold
White

To view the whole Maverick Readers scheme, visit our website at
www.maverickearlyreaders.com

Or scan the QR code above to view our scheme instantly!

Quiz Answers: 1b, 2c, 3b, 4c, 5a